Minds

Simple Tips to Improve Your Mindset and Refocus For a Positive and Growth-Centered Mind

Table of Contents

Introduction

Chapter I: Two Mindsets: Fixed versus Growth

Chapter II: Mindfulness for the Growth Mindset

Chapter III: Growth Mindset and Intelligence

Chapter IV: Growth Mindset and Happiness

Chapter V: Growth Mindset and Relationships

Conclusion

Introduction

Do you want to unleash your full potential? Are you in need of help on how to become the best version of yourself? If you do, then this is the right book for you!

Discover the different techniques and strategies on how to develop the growth mindset, the key to unlocking your full potential and learn habits for overall success and improvement. Learn to let go of the fixed mindset that holds you back from experiencing life to the fullest. Find out how to be truly intelligent, happy, creative and motivated by learning the basic principles and applying practical strategies to develop the growth mindset.

This book was written for anyone who is willing to improve their life and who is dedicated to building the right habits to achieve success. There is no better time to get started but now, so onto chapter one!

Chapter 1 - The Two Mindsets: Fixed versus Growth

The dictionary defines *mindset* as a habitual mental attitude that triggers your ability to understand and react to situations. When you entertain a particular thought repeatedly for a long period of time, it eventually takes root in your mind and becomes a part of your character.

The question you may like to ask yourself now is, *how can you describe your mindset?* Each person is likely to have a different answer because everyone has gone through different types of experiences in their life, not to mention a very unique set of genes. Nevertheless, no matter how unique a person can be, his or her mindset will still fall under either of the two main categories: the fixed mindset and the growth mindset.

The Fixed Mindset: The Stubborn Stone

The fixed mindset can be likened to a stone, because the person who has it believes that he or she only has a limited amount of personality, intelligence, and so on. In other words, your thoughts sound something like this: *I was born with these talents and this level of intelligence, so I will just work with what I already have.*

When you have a fixed mindset, you focus too much on trying to prove yourself to others with the goal of gaining confirmation. To gain a clearer image of what a fixed mindset is like (so that maybe you can reflect on it and compare your own with it), here are some situations and how it will normally react:

Whenever you are pursuing a goal:

The Fixed Mindset Reaction: *Will I look talented and smart if I achieve this goal? If so, I must never fail!*

Whenever you face an unexpected obstacle to your goal:
The Fixed Mindset Reaction: *This is beyond my abilities, so I should just give up. Besides, this is (someone else)'s fault, not mine!*

Whenever you receive a constructive feedback:
The Fixed Mindset Reaction: *I don't care what (critic) says because this is who I am and who I will always be!*

Whenever you face a challenge:
The Fixed Mindset Reaction: *I should not even consider this challenge. How do they expect me to overcome something that will only cause me to fail?*

Whenever you see someone who has achieved something:
The Fixed Mindset Reaction: *I hate (successful person)! He/She's not as talented or as intelligent as me! I should tell the others about the time when he/she (failed at something), so that that won't think he/she's* that *awesome.*

Whenever you are working with others:
The Fixed Mindset Reaction: *It's always so difficult to cooperate with those who don't agree with my ideas! I would much rather work alone than have to deal with them!*

In the end, a person with a fixed mindset will not be able to move past what he or she is now and consequently live a life below his or her full potential. If you feel that you are someone who has a fixed mindset, do not lose hope. The moment you have recognized and accepted this reality, you can start to build the right habits and move on from having a fixed mindset to a growth mindset.

The Growth Mindset: The Thirsty Sponge

Can you look back at a time when you made an effort to improve on something? If you can, try to recall as much detail about that moment as possible. Notice how you felt when you faced the challenge and the thoughts that were in your mind. Did you overcome your fear of failure? Did you focus on the learning experience instead?

By cultivating the growth mindset, you can transcend from the fluttering feelings of being self-conscious to embracing the challenge of learning and growing from whatever situations life presents to you. Your mindset becomes a sponge that absorbs openly and readily because at its core is the desire for growth. To paint a better picture of how a growth mindset deals with situations, take a look at how it reacts to the following scenarios:

Whenever you are pursuing a goal:
The Growth Mindset Reaction: *I'm so excited to give this my best shot! The best part is that I can enjoy the process as much as the achievement itself!*

Whenever you face an unexpected obstacle to your

goal:
The Growth Mindset Reaction: *I must be persistent for the sake of my goal. There is always a solution to a problem and it is up to me to figure it out! Besides, I can always change the plan, but I should never change my goal.*

Whenever you receive a constructive feedback:
The Growth Mindset Reaction: *I'm interested to find out what other people can see in me that I don't. I wonder how I can improve based on what (critic) has said about me.*

Whenever you face a challenge:
The Growth Mindset Reaction: *I hope I can learn a lot from this challenge. After all, it is an excellent opportunity for me to grow!*

Whenever you see someone who has achieved something:

The Growth Mindset Reaction: *I am so inspired and happy for him/her! They have proven that something can be done, which means that I can learn from their experience.*

Whenever you are working with others:
The Growth Mindset Reaction: *I like being exposed to different personalities so that I can learn how to work with them.*

The best part about having a growth mindset is that you never stop learning, growing and achieving. This is because you are able to love and appreciate each opportunity that presents itself, enabling your mind to open up to any learning experience that comes with it.

Changing your Mindset for the Better

People with a fixed mindset may think that it is impossible for *old dogs to learn new tricks,* but the truth is that your mindset is simply your *belief,* and that you have to power to change your beliefs the moment you acknowledge the fact that you have a choice.

Pause for a moment and consider the following scenario: you are being called in front of a large audience to answer a trivia question, and you are not prepared at all for it. Naturally, you will feel nervous as you walk towards the spotlight. As someone who may be inclined towards a more fixed mindset, you may even think, *am I going to embarrass myself in front of all these people? They will think I'm stupid for not knowing the answer! I'm going to regret this for the rest of my life.*

Now imagine another voice, a strong and confident one, inside your mind telling you, *stop thinking so negatively and just accept the challenge! If you don't know the answer, just shrug and give yourself a pat on the back for trying. On top of that, you get to learn something new when they tell you what the correct answer is. It will be a win-win situation.* With this strong voice giving you the confidence that you need, you may even be able to think more clearly and give the right answer after all. Even if you don't, you will never feel half as bad as how a person with a fixed mindset would.

While it does take constant conscious effort to develop a growth mindset, it always starts with believing that you have a choice. In the succeeding chapters, you will learn the different strategies on how to achieve this mindset so as to reach your full potential.

Chapter 2 - Mindfulness for the Growth Mindset

If there is one basic strategy that you can apply to jumpstart your path towards developing the growth mindset, it is mindfulness meditation. Mindfulness is the conscious effort of focusing on the present moment without making any judgment whatsoever. It is something that you can do anytime, anywhere.

For instance, you can practice mindfulness right now by concentrating on how you breathe naturally. Notice the feeling of air entering your lungs as you inhale and exhale. While practicing mindfulness in this moment, you do not do anything to change your breathing pattern. You do not think, *I am not breathing properly. This is not the right way to breathe.* These thoughts and actions are not the *present moment*, but rather your own judgments towards yourself.

In mindfulness meditation, the only thing you have to do is to pay attention to the one important activity that you need or want to do. For example, if you need to read a book, avoid listening to music or doing anything else that will distract you from it. If you wish to do push-ups, avoid doing it in a place where you will easily be distracted by others from doing your repetitions.

This may sound too difficult to some, especially to those who have a strong habit of self-monitoring self-correcting, but the more often you practice mindfulness, the easier it becomes for you to let go of worries and self-judgments and simply focus on having a learner's curiosity and openness. In this sense, you are on the right path towards building a strong growth mindset.

Here are some more suggestions on how to practice mindfulness in everyday situations:

While Eating

Take the time to notice the shapes and colors of the food as well as its smell. Take a small piece of the food and place it in your mouth. Notice how it feels against your tongue, its flavor and how it reacts when you chew it. Swallow and notice how it runs down your throat and down into your stomach to nourish your body with its nutrients.

While Walking

Observe your surroundings; take in the scenery, the smells, the sounds and the feel of the wind or lack thereof. Notice how the ground feels against the sole of your foot as you take your first step. Indulge in the process of walking through the area that you are in, paying attention to each new thing that you pass by. Notice how your legs and feet work hard to keep you balanced and moving forward at an even pace.

While Listening to Others

Each time someone shares their thoughts with you, listen with an open mind and let go of any personal thoughts yourself. It is all too easy to fall into the trap of just waiting for someone to finish talking so that it will be your turn to do so. While listening, really immerse your whole mind into the other person's ideas or sentiments in the same way as you would while you are listening to your favorite music or book.

Avoid finishing the other person's sentences and pay close attention to the other person's body language and tone together with his or her words. Most of all, have the willingness to empathize with him or her.

Mindful Learning for Positivity and Growth

Those struggling with focus while learning will benefit from practicing mindfulness meditation. Those who have a fixed mindset find it difficult to focus on the subject and engage with oneself because of the multitude of distractions, such as fear of failure, desire to please others, and making *looking good* to others a priority.

On the other hand, to cultivate the growth mindset one should have a learner's mind, which can be described as being conscientious of not only the subject of learning but also of himself.

How does one become a mindful learner? The first step is to identify one's reason for learning something. In other words, you ask yourself: *What is my purpose in learning this?* Once you have established your purpose, you would then have the foundation for your ambition.

The second step is to become aware of the social ties required to learn the subject. The learner must be sensitive and mindful towards his or her peers, mentor, and all other people involved in this learning process. Ask yourself: *Who is my teacher? Who are my peers? How do I feel towards them? What can I learn from them? How can I work or learn with them in harmony?*

The third step is to pay attention to the content of the subject itself. This skill takes time to hone, not unlike a muscle that needs to be worked out regularly for it to become stronger. When you learn how to focus solely on what you want to learn, you enter the mental state of flow, which is also referred to as being *in the zone.*

During this state, your entire being is completely immersed in the activity itself. Powerful athletes, bestselling writers, legendary musicians and other such individuals have learned how to put themselves in the flow state.

To tap flow, you must first establish concrete steps that you need to take towards a clear and precise goal. Next, you must understand your strengths and weaknesses so that you will know how to use them as you embark on the steps that you have established. Finally, you make a pledge to dedicate your focus towards your goal. You can even say out loud a mantra that will trigger your brain to achieve flow, such as *I am strong, focused, and ready to take on the challenge!*

Chapter 3 - The Growth Mindset and Intelligence

What are the qualities in a person that will make you think that he or she is intelligent? Is it in his or her ability to recall a multitude of facts and figures at the drop of a hat? Or is it in his or her never-ending drive to learn every day - always curious, not afraid to ask questions and finding the time to read?

A person with a growth mindset is someone who never stops learning because it is his passion to grow constantly. He knows for a fact that intelligence changes depending on one's behavior. He sees intelligence as a journey rather than as some sort of trophy or medal that will label a person's worth.

On the other hand, someone who has a fixed mindset would much rather rest on his laurels and avoid challenges whenever he can, for fear that he may fail and then not seem as intelligent to others. He views intelligence as a status symbol that needs to be maintained by making sure that others see him as flawless. He does not want to run the risk of getting low grades so he would much rather avoid the challenging subjects.

How to Develop True Intelligence?

Multiple studies such as those published in the *Journal of Personality and Social Psychology (Volume 75)* and *Psychological Science (Volume 16)* revealed that it is neither IQ nor talent that determines one's ability to perform well but rather his self-discipline. In fact, those who root themselves too deeply in the idea that IQ and talent are *innate* are often the ones who are susceptible to plateauing, or losing the motivation to learn and accept opportunities in the form of challenges.

Understand how you developed a fixed mindset view of intelligence

If you have been living your life with a fixed mindset approach towards the concepts of intelligence and success, do not beat yourself up for it because there are many factors that have influenced you to think so, especially the grown-ups in your childhood. Parents and teachers who praise children for being *intelligent* and who focus on their grades, instead of acknowledging the child's persistence and hard work, end up raising them into fixed mindset individuals.

Oftentimes, children who have never experienced defeat such as in a game or a competition also end up with a fixed mindset because they never learned how to cope with failure. Ironically, those who experienced failing one too many times also develop *learned helplessness* in that they stop trying to overcome difficult situations and instead just be passive.

You can reflect on your own childhood experiences related to the concept of intelligence, especially on how your teachers and schoolmates treated school, and how you were taught by your superiors. All these experiences and ideas others have instilled on you have more impact on your current mindset than you think, and by recognizing the root causes, you can then learn how to overcome them.

Focus on the Effort, not the Reward

The problem with most educational systems is their emphasis on grades over effort, which may be one of the biggest reasons why there are more people who suffer from a fixed mindset. Mistakes are counted and deducted from the perfect score, leading people to think that those who make more mistakes are not as intelligent.

You must train your mind not to get too caught up on the idea that intelligence is equal to the end result. Instead, channel all your energy towards enjoying the learning process. To practice, start by choosing a small goal, such as losing weight (or gaining some, if that is what your doctor recommended).

Instead of always thinking, *I must lose 10 pounds within 30 days*, you can focus on thoughts such as *I want to eat more vegetables and less meat* and *I want to exercise for 30 minutes each day.* By focusing your effort in the learning process, you will find yourself waking up each morning with the determination to choose carrot sticks over French fries and to find the time for exercise. In the end, those who concentrate on the effort are those who will naturally succeed.

View Mistakes as Opportunities for Improvement

Would it not be difficult indeed to properly tie a shoelace when you keep repeating the same wrong loops? Unfortunately, those with a fixed mindset are too stubborn to accept their own mistakes. Some would even give up altogether and just stay where they are for fear of tripping over. Those with a fixed mindset fail to see the beauty in mistakes because when one makes a mistake, one will know what *not* to do the next time around.

All the truly intelligent people in the world (and they are those who were able to discover and create new things, share their knowledge and inspire others) would agree that their mistakes helped them to achieve great things. It is their growth mindset that separates them from those who simply made mistakes and never learned from them. To have a growth mindset, you must acknowledge your mistakes and learn from them so that you can grow by not having to repeat the exact same ones.

As you can see, everyone has the power to be their most intelligent self. The moment you stop comparing your own so-called level of intelligence with others and start enjoying learning for its sake, you can unleash your full potential.

Chapter 4 - The Growth Mindset and Happiness

Fast fact: happy people are more likely to enjoy great career, greater productivity, fulfilling relationships, great health, and longevity than less happy individuals. It is for these reasons that everyone naturally is in pursuit of happiness.

Unfortunately, people with a fixed mindset perceive happiness as something that has to be achieved in conjunction with a certain condition. It is quite common for some to say, *I will only be happy once I get promoted at work* or *as soon as I can afford to buy my dream home, I will be happy.*

Those with the growth mindset, however, know that happiness can be felt in the present moment for as long as one maintains an optimistic outlook. This creates a positive cycle in itself, because when you are a positive thinker, you also become more creative, resourceful and therefore better at solving your problems. *Where there is a will, there is a way,* so they say. Because you are capable of solving your daily problems, you are able to maintain the positivity.

The habits that go with being creative and a great problem solver also enable you to enjoy working towards goals and performing well at work. Compare an individual who wakes up to a morning with a mind filled with complaints about having a bad boss and lazy co-workers, and one who wakes up full of drive and the belief in oneself that he or she will become successful.

Naturally the latter's mindset will enable him or her to be more productive and deal with different professional relationships much more smoothly. When a person is happy, his mind is full of optimism and this can give him the strength to be persistent.

Growth Mindset Habits for Happiness

Those with the growth mindset believe that happiness is a choice. Simply taking the time to feel grateful for the relationships that you have with your loved ones and the things you have worked hard to own can make you feel happy. In this light, the first habit that you should apply in your life is to practice gratitude.

You can do this by spending at least five minutes of your morning or evening reflecting on the big and little things that make you feel happy. Some people whisper a prayer of thanks, while others write a list of what they are grateful for in their journal.

The second habit is to plan ahead regularly. In general, those who plan out their day and prepare ahead of time are more confident and motivated. This is because human beings have a natural drive to be in control. After all, when you know what to expect of yourself, you become more focused.

Planning ahead is a simple habit to start. You can set aside five to ten minutes at night to create a checklist or a flowchart of the tasks that you would like to do the following day, then review the same items upon waking up. You can apply your planning skills to your diet, exercise, work and learning. For example, if you want to become a more widely read person, you can plan by creating a list of books that you would like to finish reading before the year ends. Just remember to be realistic when creating plans. Make sure that you are capable of achieving each item.

The third habit is to practice flexibility. Everyone knows that it is not possible to be in complete control all the time and that not all plans will fall perfectly into place. Unfortunately, the fixed mindset keeps you from adapting by churning out all sorts of excuses. On the other hand, the growth mindset is one that will tell you to pick yourself up, brush yourself off and learn how to deal with this unexpected obstacle with a can-do attitude.

For instance, let's say you have gotten used to studying for the exams at a particular coffee shop, and then one day, you found out that it was already closed. A fixed mindset will be irritated and tempt you to quit studying for the day because you do not have the perfect conditions that you have gotten used to. The growth mindset, however, will simply shrug it off and move on. When you are in a situation that is out of your control, you learn to adapt by changing your attitude, so you simply grab a cup of coffee from somewhere else, go to the library, and continue studying there.

The final habit that you can apply to achieve happiness while developing the growth mindset is to keep your surroundings neat and tidy. This may sound just a little bit strange, especially to those who steadfastly believe that creative people are naturally messy, but if you live in an environment where you are surrounded by the things that you love and where you know exactly where to find your belongings, you become more put-together, inspired, and happy. The growth mindset knows that the learning process goes more smoothly once the excess baggage and clutter in one's life are cleared away.

Let go of the belongings that you no longer need and want to keep in your life by selling or giving them to those who do, learn to enjoy the process of tidying up regularly, and most of all, make the most important things serve as the focal point of your space. Imagine being able to see the smiling faces of your loved ones in a picture frame hung up on a clear wall in a clean room. This alone can motivate you to become even more productive while also bringing joy into your heart.

Chapter 5 - The Growth Mindset and Relationships

Regardless of whether you are an introvert, an extrovert, or a little bit of both, you need to interact with other people to live a healthy and balanced life. It is strange to think that interpersonal skills were never really taught in detail at school back then, when it is something that everyone should be great at. The grown-ups must have assumed that you can learn it on your own as you interact with your classmates, teachers, and so on. Fortunately, there is a growing concern among researchers and educators for Emotional Intelligence or EQ, and a healthy EQ is crucial to the growth mindset.

Your mindset is what triggers you to interpret another person's words, behavior, and other communication cues, and it is what influences your means of interaction with them as well. People with a fixed mindset may say that they constantly suffer from being in *complicated relationships* when in fact they are part of what makes the entire arrangement complicated in the first place. For instance, the fixed mindset may think that if a relationship requires effort to maintain then it is not meant to be, that opposites attract, that both must agree on everything for it to work out, and other so-called *rules*.

Treating others as mind-readers, blaming the other for his own flaws, and worst of all, treating the other with contempt are just among the difficult habits of those who have a fixed mindset.

How to Apply the Growth Mindset in Relationships?

Do you believe that emotional intelligence can be improved through conscientious effort? If you do, then congratulations, because you are on your way to developing a growth-centered, positive mindset. It is important to constantly reflect on your own thoughts and feelings before you say or do anything to or for another person. This way, your relationships with others and with yourself will deepen and improve.

The first step is a difficult one, and it is to recall a time when someone hurt you. The relevance of this step is that it allows you to immerse yourself in a memory or a situation when your emotions are raging, so that you can reflect on what you have learned from it.

For instance, let's say your lover cheated on you and left you for the other person. Did you think that you should never trust in anyone ever again after that? Did this way of thinking affect how you deal with other potential love interests in the future? Now think of the same situation from the perspective of having a growth mindset. Can you forgive your ex-lover and let go of your own feelings of distrust?

The next step is to visualize the perfect partner for you, or someone whom you are physically, emotionally and mentally attracted to. Imagine being in a relationship with this perfect partner. Do you think that you two will be facing problems or is your life with that person going to be a routine of bliss? Naturally, problems will always surface in any relationship, no matter how perfect it seems. In fact, these issues can be a good thing for these provide an opportunity to establish a stronger bond.

Identify the skills you need to hone in order to deal effectively with the issues that you will face in any relationship. Some of the most powerful skills to learn are being able to listen wholeheartedly, developing empathy, patience, and being caring.

The third step is to learn how to communicate effectively. Your choice of words will make a world of difference that can make or break your relationship. In a way, it is universal knowledge that thoughts lead to words, and words lead to action, and all of these are forms of energy. Each person has the gift of releasing his or her thoughts into the world as energy in the form of words and actions, and if you maintain a generally negative mindset, you will naturally release negative energy as well.

For example, you will notice the difference between saying *You should stop ignoring me after we fight because I hate it!* and *I just want you to know that I feel bad when you don't talk to me whenever something's wrong.* While the message is essentially the same, the other person's reaction in each scenario will be entirely different, especially if you apply a more irritated tone in the former and a softer tone in the latter.

All in all, be mindful of how you interact with others by always taking the time to think before you speak or do anything. Allow yourself at least ten minutes away from a heated confrontation between yourself and another person. That way, you can calm yourself down, reflect deeply on what to do, and be able to maintain a healthy and happy relationship.

Conclusion

Hopefully, you were able to gain a clear understanding of the growth mindset and learn the different steps that you can take to achieve your full potential and live a happy life.

Nevertheless, it is still up to you to change your habits and develop the growth mindset. Don't worry, for it is never too late to enjoy true intelligence and happiness because anyone can learn something new at any age. What matters is you believe in yourself.

Finally, if you enjoyed this book, then I'd like to ask if you'd be kind enough to leave a review for this book on Amazon. It'd be greatly appreciated!

Thank you and good luck!

Printed in Great Britain
by Amazon